The
WONDROUS
Mystery

AN UPPER ROOM ADVENT READER

Compiled by Benjamin Howard

UPPER
ROOM BOOKS®
NASHVILLE

Cover design: Bruce Gore
Cover image: Wang, Elizabeth, *Mary and Joseph Look with Faith*, Private Collection © Radiant Light/Bridgeman Images
Interior design: PerfecType | Nashville

Print ISBN: 978-0-8358-1889-6 | Mobi ISBN: 978-0-8358-1891-9 | Epub ISBN: 978-0-8358-1892-6

Printed in the United States of America

Contents

Introduction

B ehold a new and wondrous mystery!" Those are the first words from St. John Chrysostom's sermon on Christmas morning. It's such a beautiful way to phrase the meaning of Christmas and the Advent season that leads up to it. It's exciting, it's filled with anticipation and awe and joy, but it's also mysterious. It's the place where the dark meets the light, where the simple meets the complex, where peace and strife stand side by side. The Savior of the world is born, but he is a child. The King who will rule lies vulnerably in a crib.

It's natural for us to try and resolve the paradoxes that surround Christmas and the Advent season, but to do so robs the season of its beauty and transcendence. The glory of the Advent season is that it's irrational. It shows us a glimpse of the way that God turns the world and our expectations upside down. In a season increasingly filled with events and get-togethers and family and friends, God calls us to sit quietly and wait for the coming of the Lord. In a season filled with the longest, darkest nights, we are told to wait for the coming of the most beautiful light. In a season of death, we look forward to the birth of eternal life.

Though we think of Advent in terms of the Christmas celebration, Advent itself is not a season of celebration. It is a time of waiting, a time when we challenge ourselves and confront ourselves during the deepest, darkest time of the year. It is only at the end of Advent, after weeks of searching our souls, that we celebrate birth and light and life.

Throughout the meditations in this book, I invite you to sit with the paradoxes that make up the Advent season. I pray that you live in the tension between light and darkness, peace and strife, solitude and community, simplicity and complexity. In the process, I hope that these writings challenge you to reflect on the new and wondrous mystery of God and the profound way that Jesus' birth flips the world as we know it and signals the beginning of God's kingdom.

In the name of the One who dwells in the paradoxes and turns the darkness into light, this is my prayer. Amen.

—Benjamin Howard

WEEK ONE

LIGHT *and* DARKNESS

Let There Be Light

Read Genesis 1:1-5

God said, "Let there be light"; and there was light. And God saw that the light was good; and God separated the light from the darkness.
—Genesis 1:3-4

"Let there be light." These words became a family code word for us when we heard a storyteller share an Iroquois tale about how the animals in the forest held a council to decide if they should have light in the midst of an all-dark world. This pretime story offered two main characters with opposing opinions.

Bear adamantly growled, "We must have darkness." This put an end to most discussion since Bear, by virtue of its size and gruffness, carried a lot of weight in the council of animals. But young Chipmunk, undaunted by Bear's power, bravely sang out, "Let there be light," again and again until the sun actually spread its gleam throughout the forest world.

There has been a stark contrast between the darkness and the light since the Creator first placed light in the sky to overcome the total darkness of the universe. But the bottom line comes down to two passages that have a cause-effect relationship: "The Word was the source of life, and this life brought light to people. The light shines in the darkness, and the darkness has never put it out" (John 1:4-5, GNT). And because of this, "You yourselves used to be in the darkness, but since you have become the Lord's people, you are in the light. So you must live like people who belong to the light, for it is the light that brings a rich harvest of every kind of goodness, righteousness, and truth" (Eph. 5:8-9, GNT).

I share with each of my children my faith that God is ultimately in charge of the world. I also share with them the reality of this world's present darkness in some of the forms it takes. This doesn't mean detailing the gruesomeness of extremist murders, but it may mean explaining that, "There are some people who kill other people." Rather than leaving my children frightened and powerless in the face of such killing, I share with them the strength that comes as we pray together for the murdered and the murderers.

Darkness comes in many guises from the violence in the world to the bullying Bear's conviction that we must have darkness. To all forms of darkness, let us sing liltingly, gaily: "Let there be light."

Anne Broyles, adapted from "Let There Be Light," *Weavings: A Journal of the Christian Spiritual Life* I, no. 2 (November/December 1986): 30–33.

Reflect

What daily practices help you remember that, despite the darkness, there will always be light?

Pray

God, you have been present since before the beginning of all things, and you are present with us in both the light and the dark. Help us remember that even when the dark seems impenetrable, you will always return us to the safety of the light.

Life Finds a Way

Read Deuteronomy 30:15-20

I have set before you life and death, blessings and curses.
Choose life so that you and your descendants may live.
—Deuteronomy 30:19

The early mornings were worst—that time just before the gentle light of dawn eases through the darkness. Those precious moments when I had usually been most centered, most creative, most prayerful, now became the most painful. I woke trembling, alone in my terror, alone in a darkness that seemed to hold no hope of dawn, alone in the heavy weight of the unknown.

"Tears are a sign of the presence of God," an early Christian writer asserted. Tears I knew well. And in my tears, I came to know the compassionate God. As a child in Sunday school, I had heard stories of a loving God. Now in my pain, that God of love was touching me and melting away old images from my heart.

"I have set before you life and death, blessings and curses. Choose life so that you and your descendants may live" (Deut. 30:19). *But how do I choose life*, I wondered, *when all I feel is death?* Yet life with its constant signs of God's loving presence mysteriously surrounded and sustained me. In a letter to friends, I wrote:

> In the midst of the grief that produces such soul-wrenching cries at times, I am still able to grasp those small affirmations of life—a beautiful sunset, brilliant red and gold leaves, the soft and warm autumn air. I cling to them as a sign of hope.

These small hints of hope gently nudged a tiny seed from that faded flower of my life. It dropped silently into the rich, dark humus of suffering in preparation for life to come. Even while weighted with death, life subtly stirred within me and I risked choosing life.

A new self—a truer self—was being revealed. Sometimes I longed for my old life simply because it was familiar, not because it was good. Choosing death seemed easier than choosing life because death was familiar; life was not. I did not move toward life confidently or easily. I stumbled, I fell, but I did move on in spite of and because of the pain. Broken and vulnerable, I feared being wounded again, but the possibility of new life—good, new life—gave me courage to push through the darkness to the light.

Jean M. Blomquist, adapted from "Of Seeds and Suffering: Growing Spiritually through a Divorce," *Weavings: A Journal of the Christian Spiritual Life* IV, no. 3 (May/June 1989): 6–14.

Reflect

When have you been given the opportunity to choose life during a time of suffering and darkness?

Pray

God, we know that life involves both light and dark, pleasure and pain. As we endure both the good and the bad, strengthen us to see the beauty and the goodness that you provide for us in all situations.

Let Our Eyes Be Opened

Read Matthew 20:29-34

They said to him, "Lord, let our eyes be opened."
—Matthew 20:33

The blind men who cry out to Jesus along the Jericho road voice a desire that wells up from the deepest reaches of the human heart. Immersed in the darkness of life's hard certainties and tormenting uncertainties, we long to see a larger truth and more encompassing purpose illuminating our years. The cry of the people of Israel echoes our own yearning: "O that we might see some good! Let the light of your face shine on us, O LORD!" (Ps. 4:6). After a lifetime of walking past undetected meaning, unnoticed opportunity, unrecognized assistance, we are aware that often we look but do not perceive, observe but do not understand. (See Isaiah 6:9.) Drowsy with the weight of daily duties and cares, we can sympathize with Jacob when he awakens from sleep to declare, "Surely the LORD is in this place—and I did not know it!" (Gen. 28:16).

God is in this place with us—that is the good news of Christmas. In the Incarnation, the light of God's countenance shines upon us from the face of the newborn in the manger. But the spiritual challenge of Christmas and the four weeks of Advent leading to it is the summons to ready ourselves for a vision of God in our midst. "Stay awake," the Gospel counsels (see Matthew 25:13), for we do not know when that holy light will meet us in the people and events around us. How can we remain spiritually awake when so much in our overstuffed culture seems to dull the consciousness of even the most intrepid seeker? How can we be alert for God's presence in the limited-visibility world of everyday life?

Jesus said, "Blessed are the pure in heart, for they will see God" (Matt. 5:8). Like all else in Christian life, purity of heart is preeminently a gift of God's love yet unavoidably a consequence of our response to this gift. William of St. Thierry, a twelfth-century Benedictine abbot, speaks of receiving glimpses of God and then finding that we must return to the ongoing work of cleansing our heart for vision.

As we wind our way to the infant of Bethlehem, whose heart beats with the intensity of God's compassion for us, may our hearts grow strong in love for all that God has made. As this happens, we will know in our own experience the fulfillment of a prayer written by a hermit of ancient Syria: "Grant me, Lord, at this time a mind filled with the love of you, and one that bears a knowledge of you, an intellect filled with insight into you, and a pure heart in which the light of the vision of you shines out."

John S. Mogabgab, adapted from "Editor's Introduction," *Weavings: A Journal of the Christian Spiritual Life* XI, no. 6 (November/December 1996): 2–3.

Reflect

What does it mean to open our eyes and look for the presence of God?

Pray

God, just like the blind men on the road to Jericho, we ask you to open our eyes so that we might see your glory and worship you.

Out of the Shadows

Read Isaiah 9:2-4

The people who walked in darkness
have seen a great light;
those who lived in a land of deep darkness—
on them light has shined.
—Isaiah 9:2

Once upon a time there was a man who lived in the middle of a desert. Yet, that was not quite true. It would be better to say that he was a prisoner of the desert. You see, somehow and sometimes in the past our friend had acquired the habit of following his shadow, and only his shadow. It was a relentless and unbending compass that he obeyed completely and followed without question. Every morning when the sun came up he began walking in the direction his shadow pointed. As the sun traced its slow crescent across the sky he followed the subtle bending of his shadow.

This had been going on for as long as he could remember. It was familiar and comfortable, the only way he knew. Yet he also had to admit that it often left him feeling trapped and alone. Sometimes he wondered what it would be like to face the sun instead of always turning his back to it and walking the other way.

Then one morning, while it was still dark, as he was preparing to set out again, something came and spoke to him. It was a voice. It said, "JUST STOP IT." That's all, "JUST STOP IT."

About this time the sun came up, and with it the powerful tug of his growing shadow. He tried to resist it but could not. Yet all that day, even as he obediently followed his shadow, the memory of the Voice and the experience of the morning stayed with him.

Then one morning, just a moment before dawn, he suddenly turned his back to the dark, western horizon and faced the glow in the east. It was done almost before he realized what he was doing. The freedom to do it happened in a moment. The rising sun in front of him was brighter and more wonderful than he had imagined anything could ever be.

Finally, one morning, the Voice came again. The gift this time was a sense of direction.

Slowly, he put one foot in front of the other, fixed his gaze on some distant mountains, and set out. He wasn't sure where he was going, but at least he wasn't still going around in circles. And he certainly didn't feel alone anymore.

David M. Griebner, adapted from "Shadowbound," *Weavings: A Journal of the Christian Spiritual Life* VI, no. 2 (March/April 1991): 32–33.

Reflect

Why is it so difficult to break from routine and embrace the freedom we are given by God?

Pray

God, you speak to us even when we do not know your name. Let us hear what you have to say and embrace your direction even when it makes us uncomfortable.

Dawn

Read John 20:1

*Early on the first day of the week, while it was still dark, Mary Magdalene
came to the tomb and saw that the stone had been removed from the tomb.*
—John 20:1

I am not by nature a morning person
I wonder at those who rise
To meet the Lord at dawn.
I wrestle with the world
And pray that God will
Keep the faith.
I walk the night streets
And wonder that God
Still spreads the feast,
And Jesus burns
The midnight oil of grace.
But as my age instructs my heart,
I sometimes pass the midnight
Boundary between expectation and prayer
And slip into the silent hours
Of waiting, the provinces of watchfulness.
Then God settles in beside me
In the dawn's October cool,
The harvest of contemplation.
I feel the Spirit's insinuation
That what I am not by nature

I shall be, by God!
And I yearn to meet
More than I know.
In the dawn drawn dew,
The Lord throws off
The rock of the night's oppression
Drops down yet again,
Lights upon this world,
Gathers what can only be,
The remnants of possibility:
The wounded hip, the pierced side,
The scarred hand, the chastened fantasies,
The mind's delight, the dance renewed,
The peace that passes understanding,
The Gideon's fleece of grace.
And I am raised
To meet the Lord
At dawn.

H. Frederick Reisz Jr., "Dawn Drawn," *Weavings: A Journal of the Christian Spiritual Life* VII, no. 4 (July/August 1992): 39–41.

Reflect

When are you most prone to encounter God? Why?

Pray

God, thank you for meeting us in the beautiful places. Thank you for showing us who you are and embracing the hope and peace of each new day.

A World of Light and Dark

Read Genesis 1:31

God saw everything that he had made, and indeed, it was very good.
And there was evening and there was morning, the sixth day.
—Genesis 1:31

and if I
  should slip away
    a quiet exhalation in time
    a moment welling up on the edge of always
      trickling without sound or regret
  into darkness of new birth
and if I
  let go of your hand
    forsaking the tenderness of flesh and eye
    for uncharted embrace
will you smile?

Neva Thorn Perdue, "At Dark's Edge," *Weavings: A Journal of the Christian Spiritual Life* V, no. 5 (September/October 1990): 33.

Light emerges gingerly
pushing the mottled night comforter
aside.
Bending the stillness,
calling forth winds,
light fully awake
tosses trees behind my head
into alluring dances on the wall I face.
And I barefoot return
grateful salutations.

Ruthann Knechel Johansen, "Morning Grace," *Weavings: A Journal of the Christian Spiritual Life* VII, no. 6 (November/December 1992): 12.

Reflect

Why is remembering that God is present both in the light and in the dark important?

Pray

God, we want to make you simple, but you refuse to be only one thing. We find you in the dark and in the light. We find you in the day and in the night. Be with us forever and remind us of your presence whenever we meet.

Death and Imagination

Read Romans 12:1-8

Do not be conformed to this world, but be transformed
by the renewing of your minds.
—Romans 12:2

Death is an assault on human sensibilities. Whether it comes by overt marauding or insidious stealth, death affronts us with its terror, greed, and shameless audacity. It takes captive our thoughts, leading them away to a fearful land of loss and pain. For Christians there is perhaps an added offense in death's advent. Biblical faith acknowledges death's reality but denies its potency. Life, not death, is God's fundamental desire for all created beings. Jesus says, "I came that they may have life, and have it abundantly" (John 10:10). God is God not of the dead, Jesus teaches, but of the living. (See Mark 12:27.) Death roughly thrusts itself between us and the vision of life we embrace in faith. It blocks our view and cynically challenges the truth of all we believe about the trampling down of death and the victory of the cross.

How can we see through death's pretensions to God's domain of light and life? It takes imagination. But human imagination as such does not fare well in the Bible. Imagination is the source of false prophecy. (See Ezekiel 13:2.) The "art and imagination of mortals" cannot yield true images of God. (See Acts 17:29.) Imagination lodges in the innermost part of our being where its potential for evil intentions or foolish ideas is laid bare by the piercing discernment of God's Word. (See Hebrews 4:12.) But what if imagination's powerful potential for misleading us were reconfigured by the mind of Christ, which Paul boldly claims we possess? (See 1 Corinthians 2:16.) Armed, as was the mind of Christ, with stories, images, and hopes drawn from God's history with the people of God, imagination can become a penetrating force that bears our vision beyond the frightful evidence of death's ascendancy to the wider reality of God's realm, bright with life. This is the hallmark of faithful imagination, which theologian Garrett Green defines as "living in conformity to the vision rendered by the Word of God in the Bible."

"Do not be conformed to this world," Paul exhorts the Christians in Rome, "but be transformed by the renewing of your minds, so that you may discern what is the will of God—what is good and acceptable and perfect" (Rom. 12:2). Here is a call to live with an imagination formed through participation in the mind of Christ. As we heed this call in the coming new year, may our capacity to see God's will for us and our world offer transforming insight into the fraudulent sovereignty of death's insistent presence.

John Mogabgab, adapted from "Editor's Introduction," *Weavings: A Journal of the Christian Spiritual Life* XII, no. 1 (January/February 1997): 2–3.

Reflect

What does it mean to confront death with "faithful imagination?"

Pray

God, you bring us peace in the middle of strife, light in darkness, and life from death. Inspire us to imagine a world where your power always transforms us.

WEEK TWO
PEACE *and* STRIFE

A Realistic Peace

Read Ephesians 2:15-20

*He came and proclaimed peace to you who were far off
and peace to those who were near; for through him both
of us have access in one Spirit to the Father.*
—Ephesians 2:17-18

There may be no experience in the world that we want more and
have less than the experience of peace. The word is everywhere,
describing something that is desired but missing—between nations,
between people, between the good earth and its inhabitants. Chiefly we
tend to notice the absence of peace between our own ears or our own
ribs, the absence of tranquility in our own hearts and minds. However
much we hanker for peace, we have for the most part learned to live
without it. The best most of us can do is to steer our ways through the
perilous waters of division and dissent without hitting too many of their
floating mines. But the avoidance of conflict is not the same thing as
the presence of peace, and that is a truth we carry down in our bones.

Because we know so little about peace, it is hard to say what is
missing: a sense of well-being, an inner purpose, an abiding calm? I
am something of an expert in the pursuit of such virtues, a veteran of
diverse efforts to achieve them. I have meditated twenty minutes a day,
run twenty miles a week, done good deeds, prayed good prayers; I have
reaped the benefits of psychotherapy and massage therapy and a few
other therapies in between, but throughout it all what I have not done
is gain any lasting hold on peace. Meanwhile the world continues to
crank out its quota of strife, flattening my hard-won serenity in its path.

The ways we have learned to speak about peace do not help me in my dilemma. To hold one's peace means to be quiet, to keep the peace means to obey, to make peace means to surrender, and to rest in peace means, after all, to die. Given these choices, is it any wonder that we feel some ambivalence about whether we want this kind of peace in our lives?

Clearly, a Christian understanding of peace means more than placidity on a personal level or polite resignation on a cultural level. Such simple-minded notions may even be what the founder of our faith renounced when he said that he did not come to bring peace but a sword. (See Matthew 10:34.) His own understanding of peace was a fierce and realistic one: that peace is nothing less than the sure sign of God's presence among us, the be-all and end-all of God's purpose for us.

Barbara Brown Taylor, adapted from "A Fierce and Realistic Peace," *Weavings: A Journal of the Christian Spiritual Life* III, no. 2 (March/April 1988): 6–11.

Reflect

What do you visualize when you hear the word *peace*? How do those thoughts connect with the fierce and realistic peace of Christ?

Pray

God, we know that you call us to live in peace with you, but it is a difficult task for us to achieve on our own. In our quest, help us find the peace that only you can provide.

A Lasting Peace

Read Isaiah 9:6-7

He is named
Wonderful Counselor, Mighty God,
Everlasting Father, Prince of Peace.
—Isaiah 9:6

Like the ancient Hebrews, our experience of peace may begin with the recognition of what it is not: not the restlessness that drains our days, or the fear that keeps us up nights, or the rivalry that drives us against and then away from one another. Those are all real parts of our lives in the world, but when we are freed from them—however, briefly—by the peace the world cannot give, then we know a different kind of reality. Never mind that it seems always just beyond our grasp, that we cannot attain it once and for all; its purpose may be to keep us on the move, and one moment of true peace is all the seed we need for our lives to bear fruit.

But what does that mean for us day by day? Clearly, it means no one thing. The quest for peace in downtown Baghdad will require different strategies than the quest for peace in downtown Detroit, but the vision is the same, a vision that is focused in one who was known four hundred years before his birth as the Prince of Peace, whose life shows us the way of peace, whose death shows us the cost of that way, and whose rising to life again shows us the fullness of his glory. "He *is* our peace," Paul writes (see Ephesians 2:14), and there are ways we are invited to experience that.

If we are disciples of his life, we will above all be reconcilers, seeking always to bring together those who are estranged, whether they are two children in the kitchen, two coworkers at the office, or two world leaders on the scaffolding of war. We will not rest easy with the achievement of a mere truce, which is no more than the cessation of hostilities. We may argue, wheedle, cajole, or slam doors, but we will not give up on the truth-telling—about ourselves and others—that precedes all lasting peace.

Finally, we will pray for peace, recognizing where our own power ends and the power of God begins. We will pray with the confidence of those who are doing what they can but who do not delude themselves about the sufficiency of their own efforts. We will remember the one with whom we are in covenant and rely on God to fulfill our purposes since it was God, after all, who put them into our hearts.

We were and are and shall be created in the image of God, whose will for us was and is and shall be peace, a peace that may pass all our understanding but one that is ours nonetheless.

Barbara Brown Taylor, adapted from "A Fierce and Realistic Peace," *Weavings: A Journal of the Christian Spiritual Life* III, no. 2 (March/April 1988): 6–11.

Reflect

When you imagine the peace of Jesus, what images come to mind?

Pray

Jesus, we pray that you bring us your peace quickly, and we look forward to its coming.

You Can't Force the Heart

Read Psalm 25:5-6

Lord, remember your compassion and faithful love—
they are forever!
—Psalm 25:6, CEB

The summer when I was twelve, I went to a nursing home with a youth group from my church. Frankly, I was there under duress. My mother had not heard my pleas that I be spared the unjust sentence of visiting a nursing home when my friends were enjoying the last day of summer vacation at the city swimming pool. Smarting from the inequity, I stood before this ancient-looking woman, holding a bouquet of crepe paper flowers. Everything about her saddened me—the worn-down face, the lopsided grin, the tendrils of gray hair protruding from a crocheted lavender cap. I thrust the bouquet at her. She looked at me, a look that pierced me to the marrow of my twelve-year-old bones. Then she spoke the words I haven't forgotten for nearly thirty years. "You didn't want to come, did you, child?"

The words stunned me. They were too painful, too powerful, too naked in their honesty. "Oh yes, I wanted to come," I protested.

A smile lifted one side of her mouth. "It's okay," she said. "You can't force the heart."

I tried to forget her. For a while I hated her for the rebuke. Then I passed it off as the harmless twittering of an old woman. Years later though, as I began to follow the labyrinth of my spiritual journey, I discovered the truth in her words.

You can't force the heart. Genuine compassion cannot be imposed from without. It doesn't happen simply by hearing a sermon on love, or being sent on a loving mission. How often have we set out to love the world—or even more difficult, to love some tiresome, undeserving, mule-headed person on our street—and given up, feeling exasperated, unappreciated, used, tired, burned out, or just plain cynical? The point is, you don't arbitrarily make up your mind to be compassionate so much as you choose to follow a journey that transforms your heart into a compassionate space.

Compassion, which is the very life of God within us, comes through slow and often difficult metamorphosis deep within the human soul. It happens through a *process.* The universe is designed to move stage by stage, from incompletion to completion. Now why should we suppose that God designed the heart any differently than the rest of creation? It, too, has its stages.

Sue Monk Kidd, adapted from "Birthing Compassion," *Weavings: A Journal of the Christian Spiritual Life* V, no. 6 (November/December 1990): 18–30.

Reflect

Do you agree with the saying, "You can't force the heart"? How does this affect the way you show compassion?

Pray

Thank you, God, for the compassion you show us, even when we are difficult. Help us show the same to others.

Surrender

Read Lamentations 5:19-22

Restore us to yourself, O Lord, that we may be restored;
renew our days as of old.
—Lamentations 5:21

A lfred Delp was a Roman Catholic priest and Jesuit who was arrested and condemned to death by the Nazis for his participation in a resistance group. The following is taken from his prison diaries.

What is God's purpose in all this? Is it a further lesson with regard to complete freedom and absolute surrender? Does he want us to drain the chalice to the dregs and are these hours of waiting preparation for an extraordinary Advent? Or is he testing our faith?

What should I do to remain loyal—go on hoping despite the hopelessness of it all? Or should I relax? Ought I to resign myself to the inevitable and is it cowardice not to do this and to go on hoping? Should I simply stand still, free and ready to take whatever God sends? I can't yet see the way clear before me; I must go on praying for light and guidance.

But one thing is gradually becoming clear—I must surrender myself completely. This is seed time, not harvest. God sows the seed and some time or other he will do the reaping. The one thing I must do is to make sure the seed falls on fertile ground. And I must arm myself against the pain and depression that sometimes almost defeat me. If this is the way God has chosen—and everything indicates that it is—then I must willingly and without rancor make it my way.

And so to conclude I will do what I so often did with my fettered hands and what I will gladly do again and again as long as I have a breath left—I will give my blessing. I will bless this land and the people; I will bless the Church and pray that her fountains may flow again fresher and more freely; I will bless all those who have believed in me and trusted me, all those who I have wronged and all those who have been good to me—often too good.

I will honestly and patiently await God's will. I will trust him till they come to fetch me. I will do my best to ensure that this blessing, too, shall not find me broken and in despair.

Alfred Delp, adapted from "After the Verdict," *Weavings: A Journal of the Christian Spiritual Life* IV, no. 3 (May/June 1989): 28–32.

Reflect

Where do you experience struggle and difficulty during this time of year? How can you confront or embrace these tests of your faith?

Pray

Lord, we surrender ourselves entirely to you. Sometimes our life seems easy, and sometimes it is full of struggles that are too hard to bear, but through it all you are present. We wait patiently for you to reveal yourself and to show us your will.

Now We Wait

Read Psalm 62:1-2

For God alone my soul waits in silence;
from him comes my salvation.
—Psalm 62:1

Waiting is one of the most difficult, and most God-like, parts of our experience. It is often difficult because it reminds us that we have not arrived, that we are unfinished, and that the present moment is one in which to live the "not yet" of faith. And waiting is frequently made more difficult by our fear of what may be, or our doubt that waiting will result in joy. But it is also God-like. Scripture bears witness to the God who waits again and again for the right moment to act in the life of a community or an individual, and that waiting is especially poignant as God takes flesh in the body of a young woman and becomes subject to the nine months of pregnancy. God's waiting affects us, and frequently we interpret it as inaction on the part of the Creator to whom we cry out. Dealing with the feelings generated by the sense that nothing is happening is an essential part of our growth in prayer and faith.

The Psalms are full of allusions to waiting and offer us a way to pray the distress ("waiting for") as well as the trust ("waiting on") that we feel as we live in the between times of unfulfilled hope. When life is consumed with problems or our bodies are pain-racked, we may want to pray in the words of Psalm 77:9, "Has God forgotten to be gracious? Has he in anger shut up his compassion?" for we really do entertain thoughts of abandonment.

Alongside these expressions of despair there are prayers of hope and thanksgiving as the psalmists learn to wait patiently, trusting that God still cares. "For God alone my soul waits in silence; from him comes my salvation" (Ps. 62:1). This verse expresses the confidence of one who, still aware of oppressive enemies all around, has learned to be still and quiet in the presence of the Creator who alone can save.

I find myself praying in both of these forms, sometimes asking God why there seems to be no end to the waiting, no answer to my questions, no relief from my fears. But I also pray as one who has experienced the compassion of God in the past and who finds in those earlier times of renewal a reason for trusting the future. Often the prayer of confidence and trust follows the cry of anguish, for in the expression of pain I consent to be honest with God, confessing the limitations of my faith and finding, like Thomas, that the One I thought was gone now stands before me.

Elizabeth J. Canham, adapted from "How Long, O Lord?" *Weavings: A Journal of the Christian Spiritual Life* VI, no. 5 (September/October 1991): 18–27.

Reflect

How can you help others not to despair during these times of waiting?

Pray

God, we know that you will come and make your home with us, but the wait sometimes is more than we can bear. Encourage our community as we wait for you.

Questions in Exile

Read Psalm 74:1-11

God, why do you cast us off forever?
—Psalm 74:1

In Psalm 73 the question "Why do the innocent suffer?" is posed, and Psalm 74 then takes one of the most painful examples of such suffering, that of exile. According to Hebrew tradition Asaph, the author of this psalm, is one of only four prophets who dares to challenge God in such direct terms. He asks whether the Almighty has abandoned the covenant people forever and makes it clear that not only is the chosen nation endangered by exile, but God's stature in the world is in question. The psalm opens with two questions: "O God, why do you cast us off forever? Why does your anger smoke against the sheep of your pasture?" (Ps. 74:1). The image of God as Shepherd of Israel (see Psalm 80:1) seems incompatible with the current experience of exile, especially since God appears to *remain* angry with the sheep, unlike the human shepherd who, though he may strike the sheep to keep them on a safe path, does not continue to administer blows.

The Hebrew scriptures frequently call upon the covenant people to remember God's mercy and compassion and to celebrate the many saving events in their past history. Now the psalmist calls upon God to remember, to take notice of the suffering, and to see the enemy's devastation of the holy places in the land. He beseeches God, "Direct your steps to the perpetual ruins" (Ps. 74:3), which may not only be an invitation to come and look at the destruction of the place where God and Israel convene but also a request that God trample and crush the enemy who now gloats over this aggression. He cries out in anguish: "How long, O God, is the foe to scoff? Is the enemy to revile your name forever?" (Ps. 74:10), and he longs for God to take out the hand, symbol of initiative and power, from its hiding place.

Exile means disorientation and a loss of equilibrium for which we all long. It compels us to ask the most fundamental questions about who we are—questions that are easy to avoid if we cling to the familiar. Few of us experience exile in such a dramatic way as the people of Judah, yet we all have to deal with losses, with changes that leave us feeling rootless, and with seasons of our lives in which God seems no longer to be listening when we cry out for help. It is in those times that the Psalms can help us give voice to the anguish and lostness.

For the Hebrew people, the experience of exile, painful though it was, became the crucible in which faith was refined in them and the faithfulness of God was made known to future generations.

Elizabeth J. Canham, adapted from "How Long, O Lord?" *Weavings: A Journal of the Christian Spiritual Life* VI, no. 5 (September/October 1991): 18–27.

Reflect

How does the experience of God's people in exile help you to understand the waiting that comes along with Advent?

Pray

O come, O come, Emmanuel
And ransom captive Israel.

Kingdom of Peace

Read Romans 14:17-19

The kingdom of God is not food and drink but righteousness
and peace and joy in the Holy Spirit.
—Romans 14:17

D o not be afraid, little flock, for it is your Father's good pleasure
to give you the kingdom" (Luke 12:32). To his pitifully small
circle of followers, surrounded by unfriendly religious and political
forces, Jesus announces an astonishing truth. Small though they are,
and vulnerable as sheep encompassed by ravening wolves (see Matthew
10:16), a great goodwill has gathered them into a reality far more significant than their present circumstances or size. From the unsearchable
depths of divine delight, God has chosen to give the friends of Jesus the
kingdom of heaven. The decision has been made, the gift bestowed.
That luminous realm toward which all history tends and all human
yearning points is theirs already.

This lavish gift establishes the unshakable groundwork of peace
within each person and among all persons. The kingdom of God is the
kingdom of peace because in it the conditions that generate strife have
been overcome. From the kingdom's abundance flows assurance that
God truly provides for human need more perfectly than we could ever
ask or imagine.

Jesus declares the gift of the kingdom with confidence because he
himself is that gift. He is the light shining in darkness, the face of God's
tender mercy, the way of peace, the guide for those who seek it. Jesus
knows how relentlessly the howling torment of the world tears at the

flesh of humanity, how costly the way of peace can be. Yet Jesus also knows that he is our peace (see Ephesians 2:14) and that those who are in him can live from this peace even as they join him in the unfinished work of restoring peace to the world. (See John 16:33.)

"No peace which is not peace for all," writes Dag Hammarskjöld, "no rest until all has been fulfilled." Clear-sighted and compassionate, these words call us to all that is aching and unfinished in the world. And by their tenacious hope, these words also remind us that a peace has been given for all, a rest offered already because in Christ all has been fulfilled.

John Mogabgab, adapted from "Editor's Introduction," *Weavings: A Journal of the Christian Spiritual Life* XIII, no. 6 (November/December 1998): 2–3.

Reflect

What does it mean that the "kingdom of God is the kingdom of peace"?

Pray

God, help us accept the gift of the kingdom that you offer us and bring peace to the world as it is in your kingdom.

WEEK THREE
SOLITUDE and COMMUNITY

The Gift of Solitude

Read Matthew 14:18-23

After [Jesus] had dismissed the crowds, he went up the mountain
by himself to pray. When evening came, he was there alone.
—Matthew 14:23

W e live in a world where we are made to believe that we are
what we do. We are important if we do something important;
we are intelligent if we do something intelligent; we are valuable if
we do something valuable. Therefore, we are very concerned to have
something to do, to be occupied. And if we are not occupied, we are
usually preoccupied, that is, busy with a worrying mind.

In solitude we discover that we are not what we do but what we are
given; that we are not the result of our judgments but born out of God's
love. In solitude we find space in which God can be revealed to us as
the great lover who made us and remade us. In solitude we discover
that we can only do something for others because God did something
for us; we can only love because we have been loved first; we can only
bring freedom to others because we have been set free; we can only give
because we have been given. In solitude we find that our call is not to
be occupied or preoccupied, not to be filled with opinions and judgments, but first of all to have the inner space, the inner emptiness into
which God can enter and teach us who we really are.

Therefore, the first gift of family members to each other is the gift
of solitude in which they can discover their real selves. A family built
on false selves, selves put together from occupation and preoccupation,
judgments and opinions, is doomed to failure. Only to the degree that

the members of a family allow each other to discover their real selves in solitude can real love exist. The family is the place where solitude kisses solitude, where, as Rilke says, "Solitudes salute each other."

The gift of solitude makes the gift of intimacy possible. St. Paul says, "Think of what is best for each other." When we live together in solitude—in reverence for God's loving Spirit—we can then enter into real intimacy with each other; we can then not only think but also do what is best for each other.

When intimacy is rooted in solitude, you can become persons to each other—persons in the sense of [the Latin] *per-sonare*, which means sounding through. Then intimacy allows us to sound through a truth wider than we can grasp, a peace deeper than we can fathom, a love greater than we can contain.

Henri J. M. Nouwen, adapted from "Spirituality and the Family," *Weavings: A Journal of the Christian Spiritual Life* III, no. 1 (January/February 1988): 6–12.

Reflect

How often do you allow yourself to seek solitude? What gifts can solitude offer you?

Pray

God, with you we know we are never alone. Help us as we seek to find the quiet moments in our lives and as we strive to center ourselves and constantly stay focused on you.

In the Ragged Meadow

Read Ecclesiastes 3:1-8

A time to tear, and a time to sew;
a time to keep silence, and a time to speak.
—Ecclesiastes 3:7

I sit in a bright-lit June meadow at the Abbey of Gethsemani, a Trappist monastery in Kentucky. It is early afternoon, and I have been here since morning in what can only be described as an uneasy solitude. Time is measured here in the chant of crickets and frogs, in the syncopated litany of songbirds, in the silence of tattered wildflowers. I look at the overgrown path meandering through the meadow grasses, and a few words of poetry come to me, e.e. cummings's reference to "the ragged meadow of my soul."

I, too, feel that my soul is a ragged inner meadow. But even though I yearn for this acre of solitude, some other part of me hungers for the larger world of "relevance," as if my solitude were a rarefied form of loitering. By most standards, I am not being productive, efficient, or the slightest bit useful, and I can't seem to help feeling . . . what? Extraneous? Indolent? Shouldn't I be back home working in a soup kitchen or something?

Being alone in order to find the world again sounds ridiculously paradoxical. It seems so even now that I'm here, but somewhere along my spiritual journey, I'd stumbled upon a difficult and enigmatic truth: True relating is born in solitude.

As I began to engage in solitude myself, I discovered and rediscovered my essential connection to others. Over the years, it was where I unearthed the gentleness with which I could truly love them. In solitude my social consciousness had been ignited and reignited.

So once again I sit in the meadow. Despite the voice inside that tells me I'm dawdling away hours of my life, I sit in the ragged meadow, making no attempt to leave, trying to open myself to solitude's severe grace.

Shadows seep along the edge of the meadow. I push to my feet and stand there a moment, looking toward the spire of the monastery church.

I think of that line from Edna St. Vincent Millay: "O World, I cannot hold thee close enough." It is a mystery, a grace, and yet that is exactly how I suddenly feel, like I want to lift my arms to receive the world and hold it to my chest. I think of the people out there, waiting beyond the borders of the meadow, and I'm delivered again into the sweet and burning knowledge that they are mine and I am theirs.

Sue Monk Kidd, adapted from "In the Ragged Meadow of My Soul," *Weavings: A Journal of the Christian Spiritual Life* XI, no. 5 (September/October 1996): 31–38.

Reflect

How can solitude help you to relate to others and connect with the world?

Pray

God, we seek you in community, and we seek you in solitude. Stay with us in the quiet places so that through your presence we can know others better.

In Retreat

Read Mark 6:45-46

After saying farewell to [the disciples], [Jesus]
went up on the mountain to pray.
—Mark 6:46

Although the Son of God, Jesus was like us in all things, including the experience of being surrounded by people who laid claim to his attention and energy: "Everybody is looking for you," Simon and his friends inform Jesus when they finally find him in his place of retreat. (See Mark 1:35-37.) This little scene is significant, for along with everybody else Simon and his friends are also looking for Jesus. It therefore reveals that Jesus needed to retreat not only from the world at large but also from those with whom he lived and worked in closest intimacy. So it is with us. There are seasons of the spiritual life in which we need to clear a space for ourselves amid the many personal obligations and expectations that crowd around us. Then it is time to withdraw our energy and attention from all the people who, in one way or another, are looking for us. We do so in order to gather and focus ourselves upon the One who calls us to give ourselves wholly in love and discipleship.

In Mark 1, and other texts that describe Jesus' going apart, the author indicates that Jesus' retreats are more than a temporary time-out in the midst of a busy schedule. Jesus does not retreat to the quiet places to find relief from the stress of his ministry or to replenish his spirit for the next phase of his work. There is no evidence that his retreats provide Jesus with new ideas for preaching or new strategies for evoking interest in his message. Rather, his retreats are simply there, hidden like the pearl of great price in the field of his activities.

What does Jesus do in these times of retreat? Our text is quite clear. He prays. We may surmise the nature of this prayer from the scene in the garden of Gethsemane: It involves the turning of Jesus' whole attention toward God, a coming into the presence of God to listen and to converse. Jesus' prayer is the concentration of his whole being on the will of his Father. It is a concentration that includes great attentiveness, the attentiveness of a lover, and results in great clarity, the clarity of freedom.

When, like Jesus, we regularly retreat in order to attend to God's Word in an especially focused way, then the time spent in this environment for listening will bear fruit in the many ministries of a spiritually alive life. What are these fruits? They are love and freedom, which nourish our spiritual growth and strengthen us for the work of proclaiming the Good News in word and deed.

John S. Mogabgab, adapted from "Seeking the Quiet Places," *Weavings: A Journal of the Christian Spiritual Life* I, no. 2 (November/December 1986): 37–41.

Reflect

How often do you allow yourself time alone to pray? How can you find this time during the busy holiday season?

Pray

God, our lives are filled with noise and distractions. We have so many obligations that it is difficult to focus on you. Help us find the quiet places so that we can turn our entire attention to you and your presence.

A Community of Stories

Read Luke 8:34-39

"Return home and tell the story of what God has done for you."
—Luke 8:39, CEB

The few mashed potatoes left in the bowl are beginning to form a yellowish crust, and tiny pearls of grease float on the water that once covered green beans. Napkins, plates, and silverware lay strewn across the table that, not long before, someone's hands had placed in order for a festive meal.

Young voices whisper at one corner of the table. Finally, one speaks aloud, "Gram, tell us again about when you were a girl." They have all heard the story before many times. Yet the satisfaction that comes from hearing their grandmother's voice speaking those familiar words is like sharing the most special of secrets. The voice of the teller, warm and quiet, begins, "I remember . . . ."

The telling of stories is woven into the fabric of our lives. When we speak about the deepest hurts and joys of ourselves and our families, we break into story. The stories we heard growing up—from the Bible, from the Brothers Grimm, from our parents or neighbors or friends— shape our images of who we are in the world and of the communities of which we are a part.

To know a story deeply and profoundly is to have a sense of belonging. First, we belong to the story. We have come to know and to care about the characters; we carry them around with us in imagination. An incident occurs in our lives, or a certain word is spoken in a certain tone of voice, and we are suddenly in the presence of one of those characters.

Story reminds us to which communities we belong. Family stories tell us that we are part of a community related by blood. In some respects knowing the stories is as much a part of belonging to a family as our biological inheritance. The stories that shape who we are and what we value also define the parameters of the communities to which we belong. Because we know the stories of Abraham and Sarah, Ruth and Naomi, David and Jonathan, and many others from the Hebrew narratives, we belong to the community of persons for whom these characters are life companions. Because we know the stories of Jesus and his followers and indeed claim to be followers ourselves, those stories form the persons we are and the decisions we make even today.

Michael E. Williams, adapted from "Voices from Unseen Rooms: Storytelling and Community," *Weavings: A Journal of the Christian Spiritual Life* V, no. 4 (July/August 1990): 18–24.

Reflect

What stories have helped to form your identity? What stories form the identity of your community?

Pray

God, thank you for the gift of stories that pass down the memories of those who have come before us from generation to generation. During this season, inspire the stories we tell with your own glory and love.

Homecoming

Read Mark 6:39-44

[Jesus] directed the disciples to seat all the people in groups as though they were having a banquet on the green grass.
—Mark 6:39, CEB

Storytelling is a form of the ancient communal spiritual discipline of hospitality. It is a communal process of transforming sojourners into kinfolk and strangers into friends. The voice of the story resonates from deep within the body and imagination of its teller, and its vibrations reach into the physical and imaginative depths of the listener. The images that linger on the outskirts of consciousness and the voices that continue to sound in the ear of the heart are the threads that connect us to those who have known and loved the story across the ages. To be invited into the world of a story is to be offered the hospitality of the community of people who live by that story.

To tell the stories that form us in the faith is to invite persons to the banquet of the word. It is to create spaces, the worlds of the stories, in which the sojourner can stop and feast. In a number of cultures the telling of stories is associated with meals. The Seneca people say that one should repay a good story with food; one nourishes the soul while the other nourishes the body. Even in the age of television, if stories are told anywhere, they will most likely be told at the table. The responsibility for telling the stories does not belong to one member alone but is passed around the table. Each teller contributes a fragment of memory to the vast mosaic.

In rural areas there is a custom called "dinner on the ground(s)." Church members bring food and place it on long tables, usually outdoors, where people will gather to feast after the church services. Former church members and family members who live far away are invited back for "Homecoming." Neighbors from other churches or no church are invited and often appear.

Around the table and under the trees, friends and family from the past are remembered. Stories are told that are never mentioned the rest of the year. The names of the dead are invoked and passed on to youngsters more interested in play than the past. Old songs are sung from memory.

There, on one brief afternoon amid the stories and the songs and the smell of casseroles and desserts, community becomes communion. Those barely familiar become family. Perhaps that is why it is called "Homecoming."

Michael E. Williams, adapted from "Voices from Unseen Rooms: Storytelling and Community," *Weavings: A Journal of the Christian Spiritual Life* V, no. 4 (July/August 1990): 18–24.

Reflect

What does coming home mean to you? What memories do you have of home?

Pray

God, no matter where we are, we are always welcome to run home to you. Thank you for your safety and sanctuary.

The Meaning of Community

Read Romans 12:4-6

*Though there are many of us, we are one body in Christ
and individually we belong to each other.*
—Romans 12:5, CEB

The original Christian community was formed within the matrix of shared life—both in its persecution, mission, worship, and fellowship. One New Testament term for this "sharing" is *koinonia*, a rich word suggesting many meanings—partnership, community, participation, communion. Literally it means "sharing with someone in something," and it is used to refer to sharing with God and in Christ, as well as with others.

Beyond this specific New Testament word, we need not look far to discover the *koinonia* dimension of the entire biblical narrative. In the Gospels alone we see the washing of feet, the sharing of bread, the shedding of tears; we see a stranger befriended, a son reconciled to a father, a mother pleading on behalf of her sick daughter; we see Jesus touching blind eyes and withered limbs, enfolding children in his arms, looking a stranger in the eye and asking for water, charging his closest friend with denial, sweating blood in prayer, caring for his mother from the cross.

It's no wonder, then, that when the church gathers to rejoin the biblical story in worship, the reality of *koinonia* comes to such palpable expression. We know such closeness to God and those around us when we harmonize a hymn, share the bread and cup, take each other's hand in passing the peace or saying hello, wink at a child peering over the next pew, speak our prayers of confession, wait together in silence, come to the altar rail for prayer or healing, receive a word of blessing. As we share with others in the worship of God, we become intimately bound up with God and one another in more ways than we know.

The Bantus of South Africa have a saying that illuminates the meaning of *koinonia* in worship: *umunty, ngamuntu, ngabantu* ("a person is a person because of other persons"). Such a truth regarding identity and society applies naturally to worship as well: A worshiper is a worshiper because of other worshipers, and because of the stirring presence of God in that worship. The first fruit of our worship, then, is the intimate sharing with God and others in the very doing of worship, whether it be a hymn that we share, a cup, a prayer, or a whisper.

Paul Lynd Escamilla, adapted from "Something Bigger Than All of Us: Koinonia, Fruitfulness, and Joy in the Worship of God," *Weavings: A Journal of the Christian Spiritual Life* X, no. 4 (July/August 1995): 25–31.

Reflect

In what ways has your community helped to form you? How do you help your community form others?

Pray

God, all of us are formed by one another, but we are ultimately formed by our relationship to you. Protect our families, our friends, and those who belong to our communities and help us be caring and compassionate to those close to us.

The Embers of Faith

Read Hebrews 12:1-6

Therefore, since we are surrounded by so great a cloud of witnesses,
let us also lay aside every weight and the sin that clings so closely,
and let us run with perseverance the race that is set before us.
—Hebrews 12:1

What makes a saint? Extravagance. Excessive love, flagrant mercy, radical affection, exorbitant charity, immoderate faith, intemperate hope, inordinate love. None of which is an achievement, a badge to be earned or a trophy to be sought; all are secondary by-products of the one thing that truly makes a saint, which is the love of God, which is membership in the body of Christ, which is what all of us, living and dead, remembered and forgotten, great souls and small, have in common. Some of us may do more with that love than others and may find ourselves able to reflect it in a way that causes others to call us saints, but the title is one that has been given to us all by virtue of our baptisms. The moment we rose dripping from the holy water we joined the communion of saints, and we cannot go back any more than we can give back our names or the blood in our veins.

There is an ancient custom that is part of the Celtic festival of Samhain that goes like this: On the last night of the year, the night of travelling souls, after all the flocks have been tended and all the grain stored, every family in the village douses the fire in their own home, carefully saving back one ember, and carries that coal to a hillside outside of town. Everyone is gathered there around a huge pile of brush and timber. When all are accounted for they toss their coals into the heap and a fire leaps up, lighting the sky for miles. They watch it burn late into the night, their faces lit up with flame, and tell all the old stories about how they have come to be here and how it goes for them, about whom they have lost this year and how hard it is to live without them, about how precious it was to live with them but how tonight it almost seems like they are all together again.

Then when the deepest part of night is over, when the children are asleep and the fire is reduced to a bed of coals, each family nudges an ember out of the ashes, puts it in their bucket and heads home to rekindle their own peat fire before going to bed. Walking down the hill toward home, they look to be a shower of falling stars, bearing their light and heat into the world. Tomorrow will be the first day of winter, but they are ready.

Barbara Brown Taylor, adapted from "A Great Cloud of Witnesses," *Weavings: A Journal of the Christian Spiritual Life* III, no. 5 (September/October 1988): 30–35.

Reflect

Who has influenced you in your journey of faith? How did they impact you?

Pray

God, we pray for your grace and mercy, not only for us but for all those who are part of our community and all those that have come before us.

Week Four

SIMPLICITY and COMPLEXITY

Grace in Simplicity

Read Psalm 95:1-5

For the LORD is a great God,
and a great King above all gods.
—Psalm 95:3

I have offered thanks over meals only sporadically during my life, though I grew up in a family where saying the blessing was a ritual obligation at virtually every meal. Early on I embraced the blessing wholeheartedly; only later did I become haphazard in my practice of saying it.

As a teenager, a friend and I liked to create a bit of religious vaudeville around the blessing. Seated at the table of his family or mine, one of us would whisper and mumble through the offering of thanks. After the amen, the other would say in an irritated voice, "I couldn't hear you." To this the one who prayed would retort, "I wasn't talking to you."

Since that time I have participated in a wide range of blessings, from "God is great, God is good," to the Hebrew blessing over the bread. I have held hands with those around the table and have looked with neither judgment nor guilt into the eyes of others with whom I was about to share a meal. In all of these experiences I never lost the troubling sense that I was simply meeting an obligation, doing what was expected, being a good boy.

Recently my lackadaisical attitude toward the blessing has been transformed. One evening at dinner my two-year-old daughter, Sarah, thrust her hands toward her mother and me, accompanying this motion with a vigorous bow of her head. When she perceived that all was ready,

Sarah said, "Thank you food." Whereupon she threw her parents a look of ecstatic delight. Then in the manner of a teacher attempting to coach a particularly slow group of students, she said in tones that invited other voices to join in, "A-men."

What I was witnessing was gratitude in as pure a form as humans ever practice it. First, it was *simple*. Three words sufficed to express my daughter's thanks. Second, Sarah's facial expression spoke more clearly than her words of the *unrestrained delight* she took in offering thanks. This is saying grace, indeed.

Simplicity is not denial of the complications of modern life. Simplicity is not so much an outward form of speech or manner as it is the driving heartbeat that sets the rhythm of a human life. Thomas Kelly defines *simplicity* as living from "a divine Center." The simplicity that characterizes this divine center allows us to make choices among the many demands on our lives. True gratitude is born of simplicity.

Michael E. Williams, adapted from "Saying Grace: Living a Life of Gratitude," *Weavings: A Journal of the Christian Spiritual Life* VII, no. 6 (November/December 1992): 28–34.

Reflect

How can you simplify the way you express what God means to you?

Pray

God, thank you! Amen.

Wisdom of the Mothers

Read Proverbs 3:1-8

In all your ways acknowledge [the LORD],
and he will make straight your paths.
—Proverbs 3:6

Sometime during my early grade school years, my paternal grandmother gave me my own copy of the Bible. It was one of those lovely yet unpretentious King James Versions intended for lifetime use: elegant parchment-like pages, a thin rim of gold leaf etched around each, a raft of special inserts at the book's beginning, each calligraphed with titles like "Family Record of Births," "Marriages," "Baptisms," "Deaths." On the first page on the artfully designated line, my grandmother had written,

From Gunga to Wendy, Easter Sunday 1955.
In all thy ways acknowledge Him
and He will direct thy paths.
—Proverbs 3:6

When she gave that Bible in 1955 and inscribed those words from Proverbs in her rounded, clearly articulated hand, my grandmother bestowed a blessing.

Things are not as simple as they once seemed during my childhood. Now I don't just read the Bible, I engage in the exegetical enterprise. And the question of who He is and what His ways might be has become clouded by the hermeneutics of suspicion and the quest for the historical Jesus. Yet I find, when I long for Wisdom's direct approach, that I still turn in the direction of the women, the grandmothers of the faith. There is, to echo the words of one contemporary woman writer, "a deep source where my mother and grandmother and all my fore-mothers still live." I push back in time to those mothers of our shared faith who still live in the psychic substrata of our prayer. In them I find few elaborately articulated systems of explanation, few theological sum-mas. Rather, they reveal through the witness of their lives the texture and shape of God's wisdom. The recorded memory of their words is a tracing by means of which I define the outline of the way that will direct my paths.

Catherine of Siena. Gertrude the Great. Julian of Norwich. The proverbs that direct their lives are discovered in the gestures, the visions, the insights, the wisdom of these grandmothers' lives.

Wendy M. Wright, adapted from "Wisdom of the Mothers," *Weavings: A Journal of the Christian Spiritual Life* XII, no. 4 (July/August 1997): 6–18.

Reflect

What does *wisdom* mean? How does its simplicity guide you through the complexities of life?

Pray

God, you speak to us through our mothers, our grandmothers, and all who have gone before us. Let us listen to those who are wise and always seek after your truth.

On Rest

Read Exodus 20:8-11

Remember the sabbath day, and keep it holy.
—Exodus 20:8

W hat so possesses us that we can't stop until "this next thing is finished"? There are many inward factors, but there is one overwhelming outward factor that grips our inward parts: the drumbeat of the marketplace that relentlessly pervades areas of life once hallowed by a break from everyday life.

Time off from this task-oriented world is increasingly individualized rather than communal; and that time off may be punctuated by work carted about on portable PCs and beeping its way through cell phones into our leisure time. Only the holidays between Thanksgiving and New Year's still have the power to make ordinary time stop, inviting a different spirit—and that is easily overstuffed and busy.

It isn't that there's anything wrong with what *The Book of Common Prayer* calls "honorable industry." It's just that having "the next thing" always breathing down our necks eventually poisons both body and soul.

Take a break, God says to ancient Israel: a real break, an absolute break from the workaday world; not just for your sake but for the sake of the whole family and tribe—wife, servants, children, and animals as well.

The sabbath, fully observed, is said to give a person a second soul, that is, to make us twice as rich, deep, and large as we were at the end of the work week. That is the reward of rest and renewal.

It's hard to describe the resonance—an inaudible but virtually physical hum that begins to emerge in a group that has entered into such separated, protected, sheltered time and space. Perhaps it is simply that the ageless rhythms of body time begin to predominate over the jerky, forced physical reactions of our increasingly pressured work time. Perhaps it is that the deep inner self, the soul, has a chance to breathe, connect, and be in touch, when not measured out by the slots in an appointment book. Or, perhaps, it is simply true that, given half a chance, some space to dwell among us, and an actual invitation, God's nearer presence settles in for a visit.

Robert C. Morris, adapted from "Soul Time," *Weavings: A Journal of the Christian Spiritual Life* XIV, no. 5 (September/October 1999): 15–22.

Reflect

How does a simple thing like taking a break help you engage with your faith better?

Pray

God, help us learn how to rest and rest well.

Small Things

Read Matthew 6:25-27

"Look at the birds of the air; they neither sow nor reap nor gather into barns, and yet your heavenly Father feeds them."
—Matthew 6:26

Small things constitute almost the whole of life. The great days of the year, for example, are few, and when they come, they seldom bring anything great to us. And the matter of all common days is made of little things, or ordinary and stale transactions. Scarcely once in a year does anything remarkable befall us. But three hundred and sixty-five days make up a year, and a year is a twentieth, fiftieth, or seventieth part of your life. And thus, with the exception of some few striking passages or great and critical occasions, perhaps not more than five or six in all, your life is made up of common, and as humans are wont to judge, unimportant things. But yet, at the end, you have done up an amazing work, and fixed an amazing result. You stand at the bar of God and look back on a life made of small things—but yet a life, how momentous.

The works of Christ are a still brighter illustration of the same truth. Notwithstanding the vast stretch and compass of the work of redemption, it is a work of the most humble detail in its style and execution. The Savior could have preached a sermon on the mount every morning. Each night he could have stilled the sea before his astonished disciples and shown the conscious waves lulling into peace under his feet. He could have made visible ascensions in the noon of every day and revealed his form standing in the sun, like the angel of the apocalypse.

But this was not his mind. The incidents of which his work is princi-
pally made up are, humanly speaking, very humble and unpretending.
His teachings were in retired places, and his illustrations drawn from
ordinary affairs.

A life of great and prodigious exploits would have been compara-
tively an easy thing for him, but to cover himself with beauty and glory
in small things, to fill and adorn every little human occasion so as to
make it divine—this was a work of skill that no mind or hand was equal
to but which shaped the atoms of the world. Such everywhere is God.
He nowhere overlooks or despises small things.

The common spheres of life and business, the small matters of the
street, the shop, the hearth, and the table, are more genial to true piety
than any artificial extraordinary scenes of a more imposing description.

Horace Bushnell, adapted from "Living to God in Small Things," *Weavings: A Journal of the Christian Spiritual Life* II, no. 3 (May/June 1987): 24–30.

Reflect

What are three small things that you can thank God for every day? How
might this change the way you interact with the world?

Pray

God, you are present in all things, and we praise you for all your work. In particular, we are thankful for the care and love that you show us in your attention to the smallest details.

Simplify

Read Acts 2:43-47

*[All who believed] would sell all their possessions and goods
and distribute the proceeds to all, as any had need.*
—Acts 2:45

Goods come to us from unknown manufacturers, food from distant places, fuel from underground conduits. We have demanded efficiency, speed, and convenience as our lifestyles have become more complex. Most of us have little direct involvement with the living, growing things so necessary to sustain life. It is not surprising that we often lack a sense of connectedness to and stewardship for the earth since we do not touch, nourish, or see it. Increasingly, this alienation has caused us to forget our place in the total scheme of things. The cry of Henry David Thoreau, "Simplify, simplify . . ." calls us to a spirituality rooted in simplicity. His choice, almost two centuries ago, to build a rustic shelter and live as simply as possible on what he could grow or earn by his labor, led him to profoundly rich insights about the nature of humanity and what we really need.

Our alienation from the earth perhaps reflects a cultural obsession even deeper than convenience. It may be that the great energy our culture expends on speed and efficiency represents an attempt to eliminate or minimize risk. We want predictability, and where life is uncertain, we are ready to pay in order to avoid the discomfort of living with its vicissitudes. In the process we can easily lose sight of the transforming newness that takes place each time we act, like our Creator, trusting ourselves to what is unknown and different.

Our movement toward simplicity, toward a more God-like embracing of life, is therefore countercultural. It challenges the assumption that predictability is essential for human well-being. Thus it causes us to question cultural norms that demand convenient, instant, or synthetic commodities at the expense of whole peoples and ecosystems. More than that, it brings into focus a lost image of power that is not the supposed power of acquisitiveness and domination but the divine energy of imagination set free to revision the cosmos. This hopeful, active imagination invites us to live and work in such a way that God can go on saying of our world, "Behold, it is very good!" (See Genesis 1:31.)

Elizabeth J. Canham, adapted from "Simplify, Simplify," *Weavings: A Journal of the Christian Spiritual Life* V, no. 3 (May/June 1990): 17–26.

Reflect

What does the call to simplicity mean to your life? How does complexity keep you from focusing on God?

Pray

God, help us to remove the barriers in our lives that keep us from you. Show us the way to simplicity, and guide us as we work toward redeeming your good world.

Presence

Read Psalm 8:4-5

You have made them a little lower than God, and
crowned them with glory and honor.
—Psalm 8:5

The psalmist sees himself not as the center of the universe but as a small yet profoundly privileged person within it. The rest of the psalm is an act of worship praising God the Creator and exalting the name of the Holy One.

It is not always possible to be in a place where the sun rises from the ocean or gentle streams speak of tranquility and so renew our spirit. But that does not cut us off from presence to created things. A collection of objects from nature—stones, feathers, pine cones, a flower or blade of grass—is accessible to most of us. Spending fifteen minutes simply being with the object, noticing its texture and color, and allowing it to "speak" of its origin or to generate thoughts of God's creative love, may be as fruitful a meditation as long hours of Bible study. In fact, the object may well call forth biblical images and ideas that lead us deeper into prayer as we realize our connection with the earth.

The present moment provides an opportunity to experience afresh some of the joys of simplicity lost to us through the frenetic activity of affluence. Families have been deeply affected by our "instant" way of life. From the credit card to instant cleaning products and headache cures, we have been accustomed to expect no-wait commodities and have fallen into a "no time" attitude toward each other. What if we were to plan at least one family meal together each week—a celebration in which each member of the household played a part in preparation—instead of every person fixing his or her own rapid meal before rushing off to the next activity? The sacramental nature of eating together might be rediscovered in this simple event. Such a rediscovery could lead us into recognition of the holiness deep within each other that reminds us who we are in relation to our Creator.

The attentiveness that allows us to be present to nature and to each other awakens in us a sense of wonder. Here small children have much to teach us. Children are blessed with a natural sense of wonder and often become absorbed for long periods in the presence of natural things. A spirituality of simplicity will affirm children in their attention to creation. But it will also recognize the child in each of us who wants to observe, play, and live fully in the marvelous world of God's making.

Elizabeth J. Canham, adapted from "Simplify, Simplify," *Weavings: A Journal of the Christian Spiritual Life* V, no. 3 (May/June 1990): 17–26.

Reflect

What are some ways that you can be more present and attuned to God?

Pray

Let us be present in the presence of God.
Let us be quiet in the silence of God.
Let us be where God is.

I Go Among Trees and Sit Still

Read Psalm 46:8-11

Be still, and know that I am God!
—Psalm 46:10

I go among trees and sit still.
All my stirring becomes quiet
around me like circles on water.
My tasks lie in their places
where I left them, asleep like cattle.

Then what is afraid of me comes
and lives a while in my sight.
What it fears in me leaves me,
and the fear of me leaves it.
It sings, and I hear its song.

Then what I am afraid of comes.
I live for a while in its sight.
What I fear in it leaves it,
and the fear of it leaves me.
It sings, and I hear its song.

After days of labor,
mute in my consternations,
I hear my song at least,
and I sing it. As we sing
the day turns, the trees move.

Wendell Berry, "I Go Among Trees," *Weavings: A Journal of the Christian Spiritual Life* VIII, no. 2 (March/April 1993): 13.

Reflect

How can you be silent and still in the presence of God during this season?

Pray

God, we sing to you with the song of our hearts. It's a song that sometimes we can't even fathom putting into words, but it shows you all of us. Help us to sing this song and help us to hear the song that others sing, the songs beyond words that connect us to you.

Christmas Eve

Wreathed in Flesh and Warm

Read Matthew 1:18-25

*"Look! A virgin will become pregnant and give birth
to a son. And they will call him Emmanuel."*
—Matthew 1:23, CEB

It is unlike most other kinds of waiting. There is a quality, a texture
to the waiting we do during pregnancy that is one only with the
waiting we do for God.

That pregnancy and the entry of divine life into the world are
inextricably related is, of course, at the heart of the Christian message.
God became human in the person of Jesus through the person of Mary,
through this woman's willingness to open herself, soul and body, to the
divine seed that soon would flower for the redemption of the world. It
was Mary's assent to the angel's startling announcement that ushered in
a new age. It was in her pregnant womb that heaven and earth were so
lovingly intermingled, through the waiting experienced in her flesh and
blood that God was made to walk with humankind.

Like the simple young woman in Nazareth, we may be surprised,
at any time, by the intuition that we too are chosen. We are hailed to
receive into ourselves the seed that God wishes to plant there. We say
yes and the life of God begins its course of gestation in us. We become
the ground out of which the incarnate God flowers in the world.

To gaze long and thoughtfully at the experience of pregnancy, especially as it is a process of waiting, is to learn something of the waiting we do for God, who breathes and moves in us, longing to be born. Our Christian faith does not celebrate the reign of a disembodied deity but a God who is with us, a God whose presence here on earth, to use the phrase struck by poet Robert Stephen Hawker in his poem "Aishah Shechinah," is "wreathed with flesh, and warm."

The wisdom of the body is the wisdom of the soul. Divine life is encoded in human flesh. We wait for God's life to grow in us, to enter the world. The waiting can be hard. We can be spent in the process. But the mystery we live is that our suffering is also a new birth. There is really one greater and more generous life of which we are one part. Our being born into it, our allowing it to come through us, is part of the creative and redemptive process of our God.

We are pregnant. We are the place of waiting, the place of the question, of the advent. We are the womb through whose pulsing life God is born.

Wendy M. Wright, adapted from "Wreathed in Flesh and Warm," *Weavings: A Journal of the Christian Spiritual Life* II, no. 1 (January/February 1987): 18–27.

Reflect

What is the spiritual value of waiting?

Pray

God, we wait in eager anticipation for you to reveal your will. On this day, we pray for you to come and be with us again.

Christmas Day

Behold a New and Wondrous Mystery

Read John 1:9-14

The Word became flesh and made his home among us. We have seen his glory, glory like that of a father's only son, full of grace and truth.
—John 1:14

I behold a new and wondrous mystery. My ears resound to the Shepherd's song, piping no soft melody, but chanting full forth a heavenly hymn. The Angels sing. The Archangels blend their voice in harmony. The Cherubim hymn their joyful praise. The Seraphim exalt His glory.

All join to praise this holy feast, beholding the Godhead here on earth, and man in heaven. He Who is above, now for our redemption dwells here below; and he that was lowly is by divine mercy raised.

Bethlehem this day resembles heaven; hearing from the stars the singing of angelic voices; and in the place of the sun, enfolds within itself on every side, the Sun of Justice. And ask not how: for where God wills, the order of nature yields. For He willed, He had the power, He descended, He redeemed; all things move in obedience to God. This day He Who is, is Born; and He Who is, becomes what He was not.

And so the kings have come, and they have seen the heavenly King that has come upon the earth, not bringing with Him Angels and Archangels, nor Thrones, nor Dominations, nor Powers, nor Principalities, but, treading a new and solitary path, He has come forth from a spotless womb.

What shall I say! And how shall I describe the Birth to you? For this wonder fills me with astonishment. The Ancient of days has become an infant.

For this He assumed my body, that I may become capable of His Word; taking my flesh, He gives me His spirit; and so He bestowing and I receiving, He prepares for me the treasure of Life.

Let us observe the Feast. Truly wondrous is the whole chronicle of the Nativity. For this day the ancient slavery is ended, the devil confounded, the demons take to flight, the power of death is broken, paradise is unlocked, the curse is taken away, sin is removed from us, error driven out, truth has been brought back, the speech of kindliness diffused, and spreads on every side, a heavenly way of life has been implanted on the earth.

St. John Chrysostom, adapted from "Christmas Morning," *Weavings: A Journal of the Christian Spiritual Life* II, no. 6 (November/December 1987): 26–29.

Reflect

How can you express the joy of Christ's birth to those in your life?

Pray

God, we praise you for all the wonders that you provide us and for your sacrifice in becoming human just like we are. You are the Holy One, and we honor your name.